I0016612

Virtual Reality, Technology, and Therapy from the College Student's Point of View

Virtual Reality, Technology, and Therapy from the College Student's Point of View:
50 College Students Comment on the Current Uses for New Technologies

Author: Christopher Michael Esposito

Contributors: Christopher Michael Esposito, Aly Miller, Lise Ho, Jason Ng, Chelsy Gonzalez, Alexander Bouraad, Zhihua Cheng, Asfand Shahzad, Minghui Lin, Chang Hyeon Lee, Xia Lin, Nicholas Favarulo, Joe Goncalves, Haifeng Zeng, Alaina Chin, Jasmine Blennau, Aiden Daniels, Xi Ge, Kenny Zhen, Christina Dorf, Jakob Reilly, Nonie Lee, Patrick Wamsley, Cynthia Hu, Gary Love, Maria Gomez, Ashley Villamar, Jamie Mathew, Joy Yim, Yulia Huertas, Shirley Nie, Jared Oefelein, Stephanie Hahn, Klaudia Ciszewska, Chanpreet Singh, Dionis Wang, Nikki Fogarty, Betty Monsanto_, Lily Yuan, Min-Ji Seo, Minghui Lin, Alaina Chin, Andy Law, Shaniza Nizam, Laura Dominguez, Marissa Bavaro, Bridget Scheinert, Micah Baja, and Ricardo Dixon

Edited by Christopher Michael Esposito

Christopher Michael Esposito
2016

Copyright © 2016 by Christopher Michael Esposito

All rights reserved. This book or any portion thereof may not be reproduced or used in any manner whatsoever without the express written permission of the publisher except for the use of brief quotations in a book review or scholarly journal.

First Printing: 2016

ISBN: 978-0-578-18101-1

997 Ionia Avenue
Staten Island, New York 10309

Special discounts are available for quantity purchases. For details pertaining to such purchases, please contact the publisher listed above, Christopher Michael Esposito, at Tel: (917) 932-4188 or email: christopher.m.esposito@stonybrook.edu.

Dedication

To those who are distanced from society by technology,
additction, or disorder.

Table of Contents

Acknowledgements

I would like to thank my theater professor and my theater classmates, without whose help this book would never have been completed.

Thank you for your patience and guidance.

Preface

Preface by Christopher Michael Esposito

The sections of text included in the following chapters were gathered from a blog used for a theater class at Stony Brook University. The class was titled Introduction to Visual Interpretation and discusses the impact of technology on art, therapy, and society. The following texts were written by students of the course, in which, they discussed the impacts of technologies and their anticipations of what might come from new technologies in the future. All of the students consented to having their texts published in this book. As you begin reading, you'll learn about new technological innovations in virtual and augmented reality such as the HTC Vive and the Oculus Rift, which recently have become hot fields in the areas of gaming as well as therapy, since they are spearheading a new field of super-realism in the computer realm. Many of the blogs, but certainly not all, speak in high regard towards these devices and their great potential, but there are some outlying skeptics who believe that technology isn't always the way to lean towards when seeking treatment and entertainment. After the discussions of virtual and augmented reality you will find yourself learning about the students' opinions on technology and how it might impact a user's mind. The overwhelming majority of students believe that most recent innovations in technology in areas such as social media and communication hamper basic social skills. Some anecdotes are quite riveting, you just wait and see. The following chapter discusses more perks of technological advancement, particularly in the medical field. The students were quite amazed by how technology and medicine can complement each other so well that human error can nearly be extinguished from medical practice. Lastly, the students describe how technology can be used in therapeutic practices, which is quite interesting, since the second chapter discusses quite the contrary, again, you'll just have to wait and see for yourself.

Chapter 1: Virtual Reality and Augmented Reality

Christopher Michael Esposito:

For the first time, I recently had the luxury of being able to use the HTC Vive. In short, it was captivating. Everything seemed so real inside the Vive. I was in a simulation, during which, I was able to draw in 3D. I was able to draw under, over, around, and between what I already drew. In addition, the environments for the virtual realities are literally panoramas of actual environments on Earth. I believe that this device has huge potential, and the sky is the limit for its capabilities.

Some ideas that came into my mind when using the Vive were much more high tech virtual tours of colleges and vacation spots as well as psychological therapies. Likewise, video game experiences could, and will, be innovated immensely.

Christopher Michael Esposito:

Today's society lacks a major key to emotional connection-empathy. When journalists try to describe a traumatic event to their readers/listeners, they do the best they can, but oftentimes, leave their readers ignorant of the significance of the event.

For example, some adamant critics of the current police brutality firmly stand by their beliefs, supporting our state officers. However, by using a better tool to depict these events for such haters, they will have no other choice but to develop some empathy for these harassed individuals. Virtual reality seems to be the best tool to do this. By using certain computer generated images, police voice calls, and eye witness testimonies; journalists can vividly recreate the event and help immerse their viewers into the event, and therefore, help their viewers empathize.

Betty Monsanto:

VR technology were acquired by Facebook and are soon being shipped to consumers. Beats me what Facebook plans to do with the technology. Perhaps we will soon be able to virtually hang out with our friends from our timeline. However, VR technology will be costly if consumers will choice to use Amazon markets and Oculus' own shop. Of course, we should expect some competitor companies to emerge such as HTC's Vive.

My initial reaction to the VR was an upgrade to the gaming industry. I figured people want virtual reality in video games, nowhere else. However, I can now appreciate how many industries this technology can change.

Adweek brought to light many interesting predictions about how the VR will be incorporated in different industries of branding.

GoPro sees opportunity to bring youtube action videos to life with the VR. This could possible enhance the GoPro industry, the film industry in general.

British Columbia Tourism will be using VR to transport its clients to destinations

VR technology could change how brands present their products to consumers, making products more marketable and increasing sales.

Christina Dorf:

Recently, my mother got a new phone, and, because I have many family members that work at Best Buy, we received a free virtual reality device that my mom can hook up to her phone. This was my first experience with virtual reality, and it was quite confusing to comprehend; I was left both dazed and amazed. When you put on the goggles, it's like you are literally stepping foot in a whole new world. Any direction you turn, there is a part of an atmosphere that seems so realistic it's almost frightening. This experience made me wonder how big of a role this will play in our future, and just what will we be able to do with it?

Aly Miller:

In class, we discussed the amazing invention of the Oculus Rift. When my professor asked how many people have tried it, I felt out of the loop being one of the only people who haven't heard of it nor tried it out. When my professor described it to us, he described it as something that you put on your eyes which makes you see different scenes and when you turn your head, you see more. It becomes your new reality. It also connects to your ears so that you not only see this new reality, but also hear it. You become immersed in this new reality. The Oculus Rift has competition now, though. The HTC Vive has feature that the Oculus Rift doesn't: touch sensors. The HTC Vive was what the Disney artist, Glen Keane, used to make new, three-dimensional, sketches. But, the HTC Vive is more expensive at about $200 more. One of the students in my class mentioned that the HTC Vive lets players know if they're about to walk into a wall, which is a great thing to have on technology as advanced as this. While companies are trying to advance further and further, we cannot forget the safety of the people who will be buying the products. I believe my professor mentioned that there are even more companies making inventions similar to these which increases the competitiveness. I believe that these inventions will change the lives of gamers, that is, if they have the money.

Lise Ho:

Increasingly the field of virtual reality is growing due to the increase of accessibility of technologies such as the Oculus Rift and the Google Cardboard. However, as society tends to do many times, we are often informed about the great successes in this field, such as the 3-D game. But society needs to reevaluate every aspect of this technology as increasingly these technologies are being used for awful purposes.

For instance, an article I've read explains how virtual reality is being used in the porn industry. As a probable traditionalist with conservative views in this aspect, I feel that porn in general is detrimental to not only our society but also to the psyche of users of it. (I will spare you my deeply felt opinions about this matter of pornographic images and turn to where the issue lies).

As the porn industry is increasingly developing programs to simulate real sexual activity in virtual reality, the ability this will give people will impact our society's behavior. For instance, abuse of an electronic projection of a partner in virtual reality will have virtually no laws to prohibit it. However, this will promote in the psyche of the users that this is a real but also doable thing that they may choose to enact on in the real world outside the cardboard or the Oculus. Furthermore, the creation of these images in virtual space increases the hopes and dreams of a person's ideal of a partner in what they look at in their physical appearance.

I wholeheartedly feel disgust that we judge our partners by their looks, but nevertheless, we all have our preferences and bias. However, as we can always code up another vision of what the "perfect" partner can be (at least in the future), this will leave users craving these ideals that do not exist in the real world. And thus, we may end up being sucked in a vacuum where we have been exposed to a virtual fantasy that cannot and will not exist in real life. This will in turn drive people to insanity, deep lust, and depression as these impossible desires will forever be able to be repeated in virtual space but will never exist in reality. And who knows what will be a result of these unmet expectations? It would not be far to imagine a dystopia sometime in the future due to the potential negative impact virtual reality may have on our perceptions of our lives and our relationships with others.

Thus, it is important for society as a whole to recognize the potential moral issues that come with the advancing technology and to place the appropriate laws before our society transforms into one that loses control of itself.

Joe Goncalves:

As we've seen in recent years VR is drastically changing all sorts of aspects of our lives, whether it's the added immersion of a VR film to the new level of interactivity with VR gaming, it's clear that Virtual Reality is a game changer and is here to stay. With the technology being made consistently more affordable and accessible, we must naturally stipulate on its future uses, and how we can push the tech to its farthest potential.

One area that many foresee as being drastically changed by VR is the University experience. As time goes on and technology gets increasingly sophisticated, we see the current paradigm of University beginning to be less effective. With the digitation of more educational resources, the idea of living on a campus, paying an absolutely absurd amount of money, and spending hours sitting in a classroom listening to a professor seems less relevant. We're beginning to see that more and more of the University experience is easily replaceable with VR. For one thing, the use of a campus' technical resources, such as the libraries and computer labs has become nearly obsolete, as with the internet any student can find just about any information they want without having to spend hour after hour searching through books in the library, and you'd be hard pressed to find a student at a University that didn't own a computer that they could do their own work on from wherever they please. Then comes the aspect of the lecture setting. If students could get their hands on their own devices such as on Oculus Rift, a lecture could be live streamed straight to the students, without the need to go to a campus and go to a gigantic lecture hall with hundreds of other students. And with the use of technology similar to the clickers a lot of Universities use today, students could even ask questions during the lecture or submit answers for questions. The digitalization of the University experience could be a big blow to the institutions in place today, but it could be a massive financial benefit to the students themselves. We've already begun to see a massive outpour of digital education resources such as Khan Academy and Lynda.com, so it is absolutely possible that VR could bring this movement one step farther.

There is one downside I see to this possible digitalization of higher education, and that is the social aspect of University. With the total digitization of the experience, we would lose out on the social value of going away to University and learning independence, and the growth process that comes with that. As someone who has spent his entire college experience within a half hour from his house, I think it's not unreasonable to say that not getting this experience can be a huge hindrance on social and personal growth. All of that aside though, I do foresee a future where instead of getting up and driving to their campus or walking there from their dorms, students will grab their VR devices, plug in and experience their classes that way, at what will presumably be a massive economic relief for struggling young students.

Joe Goncalves:

Recently in the Royal London Hospital, a colon cancer operation was filmed, which isn't necessarily rare in itself, but what makes the event unique, is that it was the first time a medical operation has been filmed in Virtual Reality.

The surgeons had set up two setups for 360 filming within the operating room, which was then streamed live to medicalrealities.com. The process is a huge step forward in the process of teaching a new generation of surgeons. Now training doctors can see the process up close and personal and understand all the nuances of what is going on in the operating room.

It's just another way that the new accessibility of VR is improving yet another field.

Bridget Scheinert:

The media plays a large role in the society we live in whether it be how to act or what to wear. It only seems logical that VR is making big strides within media as well. In the media VR has several uses ranging from film and music to books and art. VR can be used to basically place yourself in a particular film. Some films that have been used in trial are The Matrix and The Thirteenth Floor. It gives you the feel that you are trapped in a machine or whatever the setting is. VR is also being used in music to allow composers to come up with different musical pieces using the instruments virtually. Artists are also using VR to create different works of art and experiment with different techniques or looks.

Bridget Scheinert:

Virtual reality has taken over not only the world of video games but it soon will take over our social life. Facebook is hoping to use the HTC vive for various things. Yes, virtual reality is an amazing and ever-changing concept however I think it may have some negative effects on our society. We as is hide behind computer screens and don't really interact with others as much as we used to.

Everything is digital now rarely do you hear of someone making a phone call or sending a letter. Our family time is now spent on Skype instead of in the same room. I believe that virtual reality is only going to increase the time spent alone. It is going to lead to a connected society but yet a distant one. We are going to be close with those far from us but far from those who are close to us.

Bridget Scheinert:

Virtual Reality can be used for several applications in the medical field including surgical training. VR puts a spin on how we see our world. It allows us to experience something extremely realistic while it not entirely being real. For the medical field this is a major advancement. In recent surgical practices the VR has been used to train surgeons in example surgery. This allows the surgeon to practice hands on as if the controllers were there tools and perform a surgery. They gain valuable skills while no one is harmed in the practice.

Bridget Scheinert:

Along with the many uses of virtual reality it is also being used to treat war veterans who are suffering with PTSD. The first time VR was used to help treat PTSD was in 1997 when it simulated a Vietnam War zone. It is now being used to present the veterans with situations represent Iraq of Afghanistan. This allows doctors to see how their patients react to certain triggers and what can help to prevent panic episodes. It also allows the patient to learn certain mechanisms to help cope with their trauma.

Jason Ng:

Recently at Facebook's F8 Developer Conference, Mike Schroepfer did a demo on how Facebook could use VR. The first action that he showed was the ability to enter a 360 degree photo. By grabbing a photo that was in the form a sphere and then pushing it towards the face, it makes the user see the photo in 360 degrees, like what it currently does in Facebook. Honestly, this doesn't seem too new or interesting because it is the exact same as it currently is.

Instead of clicking and dragging to look around, the user would tilt his/her head to look around, which is not amazing. The next action was the "VR selfie" in which a selfie was taken with the VR avatar. They had a VR selfie stick and used it to take pictures of their avatars with the background as the 360 degree photo they were currently using and then being able to discard it or upload to Facebook. This is interesting, but and it seems fun. The only thing that somewhat annoys me is that they are currently using the VR avatar, which is the shape of the head and the hands. There is always the possibility of upgrading it by uploading a picture to use as the face and maybe for the hands as well. Another feature was using a "pencil" to draw and then something such as a tie and then applying it to the avatar. This function also seems fun, but also is somewhat risky as some inappropriate things might be drawn. Also, without the ability to see the avatar, application of an object is difficult. There is also the function of applying a "mask" which just seems to change the avatar's color, which is basic in my opinion. Since Facebook is tinkering with the idea to apply VR to Facebook, new possibilities are introduced and allow for new and interesting interactions with friends, but currently it just seems like a Skype that allows for you to take pictures with friends and drop a background.

Jason Ng

With the release of VR (Virtual Reality) equipment, such as the Oculus Rift and the HTC Vive, a whole new realm of gaming is introduced. Being a casual gamer myself, I am somewhat excited to experience VR gaming. However, I don't think it's possible. I believe that VR gaming is a luxury. There are two reasons why VR gaming is a luxury. The first and most important reason is the cost. The price of an Oculus Rift by itself (well, not by itself but with the add-ons) is about $600 and the price of a HTC Vive is about $800. That is extremely expensive to me because most of the latest consoles are about $300 for the console. I'm not sure if there is a price for the games on the VR equipment, but there's already a $300 difference, which is pretty hefty. Not only has that, but to use the equipment, there had to be a computer with good specs, which can add to the cost. The second reason is because to fully utilize VR gaming, adequate space is needed. The Oculus Rift and HTC Vive make use of motion sensors for VR and therefore the body needs to move to use it. However, space can sometimes be a luxury. For example, in our dorm rooms, I doubt there is enough space to move around enough to use the equipment. I once saw a video where this professional gaming team was playing with a HTC Vive and they had to dedicate an entire room for it and they actually went around walking in that entire room. Although with the release of the Oculus Rift and HTC Vive allows for a new era of entertainment, it feels too much of a luxury and I won't purchase it.

Klaudia Ciszewska:

I didn't know about this gadget about I heard about it in this class, and couldn't be more confused at first. So I looked it up and realized what it is and what it meant. It is a means of putting yourself into an alternate universe. Seeing the things you could do with this, I realized that this would have a huge impact on medicine. It could be used by medical students to actually perform surgery, similar to the leap, but it would be more realistic. This gadget is amazing but could also be used for bad purposes. If spent too much using this the person could be "sucked" into the alternate world and could potentially lose sense of reality.

Betty Monsanto:

Here's the VR being used in ways I never even imagined. Excedrin® Migraine using the VR for consumers to experience migraine symptoms. The VR does this by stimulating bright lights, darkness, and frequencies in patterns that mimic migraine pains. The marketing pitch is genius. It's a common notion for patients that suffer from migraine to not feel empathy from those around them because most people do not understand how severe the pain might feel. Here is another example of virtual reality changing the market landscape and connecting users with brands in ways never done before.

Patrick Wamsley:

Very recently, the Oculus Rift, the original Virtual Reality

Headset, finally was released to the public. Is this the next big thing? It's certainly incredibly cool, and programming for it is extremely fun. The idea of virtual reality, living in and being a part of your content, is an incredibly solid pitch. Even though the technology is new, it's been fully embraced by media production, the gaming industry, and even the adult industry. There is also a massive amount of hype surrounding all of VR. It's bound to explode, at least initially.

Hopefully the technology is assessable enough to quickly reach a high market share when gen2 or gen3 is released. I think its popularity will bottle neck unless the team does a good job of marketing it to everyone who could benefit from the product; rather than it just being a really cool toy for gamers and geeks. I'm hopeful that it will take off. If it does, it will create more and more competition, which will create better and better technology, which will improve the experience and lower the cost. I'm very much looking forward to the advancements in this area that we'll see in the future. Hmm, future. That seems like a good word to describe the technology of virtual reality.

Bridget Scheinert:

Virtual Reality is taking the world by storm and it is no surprise when it will soon be implemented in education systems worldwide. One interesting way it can be used in education is studying astronomy. Students are able to virtually put themselves in the sky and learn about the locations of different galaxies and stars in or out of our solar system. It's hard to visualize such a vast part of life and putting yourself in it can be an extreme advantage to learning about it. With this new technology students can move around and study different planets or stars. In addition they can track different comets and the tracks each one is taking. This is a major advancement in education and I'm sure there is only more to come.

Bridget Scheinert:

VR is taking over the world and it soon will be the new videochat. Combining 360 cameras with Virtual Reality will now allow you to video chat with those far away with you. First the phone call is made and then it is streamed through ones oculus rift. It allows you to share moments directly in time while being miles away. This program uses a 3D camera and the oculus rift and was developed by SummitTech. This may possibly be the closest humans will get to teleporting themselves to varying destinations.

Bridget Scheinert:

Virtual Reality is going to be huge within society in several different aspects. One part of society where VR is going to be big is fashion. The fashion industry will soon be using VR in several ways. One way is a virtual fashion show. Not everyone is able to attend Paris and New York for the week so a virtual fashion show would allow designers and other personal in the industry to experience it will not exactly being present at the fashion show. The industry can also use it to allow for virtual shopping. Online shopping will be put to shame when you are able to virtually walk around a store and shop for clothes and purchase them. Virtual Reality is sure to change the fashion world.

Chelsy Gonzalez:

The Oculus Rift and Touch are really exciting. The things you can do with this is probably amazing. The opportunities are endless with these devices. One of the main things I know they will use this for is for tours. When you can't actually be there, but want to see the place, this would be perfect. I've seen many companies use the virtual reality aspect of the oculus rift, to tour different places, they have definitely benefit from it. I also seen real estate companies, use virtual reality to tour the houses. These can also be used to teach different things, which can actually save money. Instead of actually having the equipment, you can use the Oculus rift and touch, to replace the equipment, and virtual use the equipment.

Xia Lin:

3D-VR will help human to study things in the fun way. When we study something like biology, we have to remember a lot of name of cells, and every cells have their own structures so we have to remember the names of those structures. People will feel boring and hard to remember those names. We find out that it is easier for people to remember cells' name in the lab because they can see those cells in real, and they also find the way interesting. However, it is impossible to introduce every cells in the lab, so 3D-VR can help people to study the cells in the much better way. People can work in to the cells to see the whole structure inside the cells just like we become small than the cells. If this idea really into the education who will like to learn the cells in the book rather than 3D-VR.

Bridget Scheinert:

A new app developed for Google Cardboard and VR called ARTE360 allows the gamer to immerse themselves in various locations around the world. This could be advantageous for a wide variety of people. People who are handicapped and can't travel the world well this app allows them to be placed in and explore some of the most beautiful places on Earth. People who can't travel and see the world are missing out on a lot and allowing them to have this app would allow them to experience the world as it should be. Some examples of the places that can be explored are mountain ranges, old and new buildings, and several ocean scenes.

Joe Goncalves:

It's clear to most of us in the world today that VR is the next major step in technology, as we've seen numerous devices over the past decades take what once seemed like science fiction to the masses. There is a near infinite amount of uses for this new tech, but as a prospective journalist, one of the most enticing to me is the idea of virtual reality news reporting. In the 60's use of video in breaking news events such as the Vietnam rattled the world, and made people feel more connected to the events being witnessed. VR takes this principle to a whole new level.
Imagine watching a news report on your oculus or another VR device, and instead of simply seeing video footage from a camera crew on location, being put there through virtual reality and 3D video. As the use of 3D video becomes more economically feasible and accessible to the consumer, it is perfectly reasonable to suppose that it will

become the new standard in video. Now imagine being transported to a protest, or a war zone, or a political debate, all from the comfort of your home. One major part of news reporting is the connection the news consumer feels with the piece, and there is no experience quite as intimate and engaging as that which can be achieved with future 3D video and VR technology.

Alexander Bouraad:

Virtual reality is predicted to be the next big thing. Or is it the next google glasses? I believe that no human will want to lose its ability to control its life and be forced to sit in a single place while we are in a virtual reality. I think that even though we will have the ability to live in a world that is created for us, that it will never overtake the real world we live in. As of right now, none of the products that distract our vision and our ability to be in the current day and time, will never succeed in this day and age. I believe it is due to our generation's obsession with living in the moment and staying ahead of the curve at all costs.

Zhihua Cheng:

Virtual reality (VR) technology is getting us into a virtual word. I read the article " For virtual reality pioneers, no rush to succeed in 2016" by Derrik J. Lang, which is about Oculus's VR is surrounding wearer's eyes with 360 degrees in the virtual world. This is kind of an amazing technology, with an app that has all kind of background information, we would even believe our life is standing inside that virtual world. As Lang had reported in the article, the headset can detected users' movement. It also create a virtual view that would give users a virtual experience. Certain games are developing to play with using VR. I am expecting how it would feel like it we actually play those games with our physical movements.

Asfand Shahzad:

Just a couple months ago Samsung had introduced their new VR goggles. Everybody went crazy for them because it's an amazing piece of technology and it is not very expensive compared to their old

VR. As soon as it came out Amazon ran out of them. I had tried on the Samsung VR before it came out in market and I was astonished by the things you could do with it. You are in a different world when you put the goggles on. It was unlike I had seen anything before.

There are some ways Samsung could make the VR better. The quality of the video could be better. Samsung should also try to make the VR universal to other android phones also instead of it just being for specific Samsung phones. If this technology is perfected than in the future people may only watch shows, movies and play games on the VR instead of using a T.V. Hopefully Samsung will surprise us with what improvements they will bring to the VR in the future.

Christopher Michael Esposito:

In a recent Ted Talk by Nonny de la Pena the future of virtual reality was discussed. Taking most by surprise, virtual reality's new direction was towards the news. A recent struggle in the news industry lied within the area of sentimentalization. Some stories may have been truly heart wrenching, but they couldn't be articulated well with words and images, they're just some of those you had to be there moments.

With recent innovations in the virtual reality field, news reporters were able to take their viewers' experiences to whole new levels. Some experts were able to create a scene of a little girl smiling and singing on the sidewalk in Syria, then a bomb goes off. We often hear about bombings in far-away countries and know that they're bad and traumatic, but can't actually relate. This innovation in news reporting can really change the way we think about such occurrences in Middle East. These innovations can make us a little less selfish and a little more sympathetic for people who experience such dramatic events.

Minghui Lin:

Have you heard about Clash of Clans? Have you heard about Virtual Reality? How about Clash of Clans in Virtual Reality? Today, Virtual Reality is getting hotter and hotter. In today's technology, we already have had 4K TV that comes from CES 2016. However, in my option, nothing can have better experience than Immersive or 3D view. I believe that Virtual Reality comes from 3D ideas. Normally, in order to view images or watch videos in 3D model, we usually wear 3D glass and 3D style movie. The 3D glasses are easy to be made. However, 3D movies are not very easy to be made.

They required many technologies behind them. How about personal 3D view machine. How about view in 3D in personal phones? I believe that Virtual Reality is a great solution for it. Most of Virtual Reality headsets are made for phone because today's computing system is getting smaller and smaller.

Where can we use Virtual Reality in the future? I believe that they are many field. For example, projection. In the future, teachers can show 3D models in students' Virtual Reality headsets. And also students can interact with them. For example, Virtual Reality Phone Calling. Two couple can see each other in Virtual Reality like seen in Reality. For example, Meeting in Virtual Reality. Workers can wear Virtual Reality to have meeting, then they are needed to transport physically. For example, virtual travel. In the future, we can travel and visit anywhere in Virtual Reality by just sitting at home. How cool it is! Of course, if there are some flower fragrance from Virtual Reality, they will much better experience! There is an even better solution which is to combine neuro mind-wave technology with Virtual Reality. As soon as we have it, we have the world! Looking forward these technologies in the future.

Chang Hyeon Lee:

People who interest on IT product can imagine the date March 15th, 2016 is Apple's big event about launching 4 inches new IPhone and 9.7 inches new IPad. However, there is another big event, PlayStation VR launching event as known as project Morpheus from San Francisco. Every game player expects to this VR for playing game more spectacle. Its price is biggest issue among the game players because other companies' VR for game users such as Oculus rift, and HTC vibe are so expensive, many customers felt a sense of betrayal. These VR would increase the level of games and more various virtual reality.

Xia Lin:

This is my first time see the VR in class. It is very interesting, and our professor says he will get one in class. I was very excite about it. When we watched the film about the VR, the artist draw with the VR in the 2D space, he can check the left and right of the image which he draw, and also get farther and close. It is very surprise me when he walks close to the image of the roe, the roe become alive just like we see in the movie.

Nicholas Favarulo:

It's scary to think about the impact virtual reality can have on the world in the near future. Virtual reality allows you to be in a different world with the comfort of being in your own home. Instead of going on vacation to Italy, you can stroll the streets of Rome through VR. This is fascinating and should be a hot commodity for consumers in the next couple of years. I believe VR can also have a huge impact in the classroom. Virtual Reality can potentially wipe out all universities. Instead of going away to school and being in extreme debt, you can learn from one of the best professors in the world while using VR. This device could help make the world more educated as a whole. Now people who can't afford to go away to school or leave their homes can now get a quality education. Virtual Reality is starting to gain attention and will only become more well-known as the years go on.

Joe Goncalves:

McDonald's Sweden will be the first in what I'm sure will be a long line of McDonald's stores that are now creating versions of their signature Happy Meal boxes that can be folded into VR headsets, in the same fashion as Google cardboard. If Google cardboard's $15 price tag is a bit too much to indulge on, then it is only going to cost the price of a happy meal to get your own virtual reality experience. The new "Happy Goggles" as they're calling them, may just be a marketing technique, but it's still not something to scoff at, and it is going to make VR much more available, especially for the younger generation. Thankfully I already have a Google cardboard set because I really don't feel like pushing a grease saturated fast food box against my face, but I'm sure the little ones won't think about that too much.

I'm not sure what software will be available via some McDonald's VR app, but who knows, maybe they'll do something good and take you on a VR journey of your clogging arteries.
I think if there's any sign that VR is going to proliferate just about every aspect of our daily lives, this is it.

Maria Gomez:

The oculus rift is a new and very advanced gadget that allows you to be in your own virtual world just by simply putting on a goggle like piece. You can choose what environment you would like to be in and it transports you to that exact place. In class, we used a cheaper version of the oculus rift. We used a Google app on out=r phones and the headpiece provided, and I was very amazed when I put it on. I was in Paris and I was directly in front of the Eiffel Tower. Everything looked extremely real and my orientation would change as I moved my head in different directions.

Ashley Villamar:

2016 is the year that Virtual Reality is going mainstream. VR is currently popular for the gaming industry; however, it has the potential to have a much more meaningful impact for the masses if it is used towards enterprise. Real estate, medicine and manufacturing are just a few areas that have already seen the benefits of virtual reality. VR's potential in real estate is having the power to present finished models to client even when the actual, physical fixture is not completed yet. Virtual reality provides instructional content for healthcare professionals, as well as patients. With the help of VR surgeons can practice rare and complicated surgeries and patients have the ability to learn and understand everything about their operations and recoveries.
The manufacturing business is saving money by designing and innovating with 3D, VR, models rather than physical prototypes. I think that VR is going to have an enormous impact on society starting this year. It is very important that we advocate and encourage VR advancement not only in the gaming industry but in the enterprise. Instead of fearing the rise of virtual reality we must embrace this advancement in technology and take advantage of all the

incredible features it has to offer us.

Ashley Villamar:

Fox Sports and NextVR are collaborating to stream the NCAA's March Madness Tournament in virtual reality. The tournament will be held and recorded at Madison Square Garden in New York City. Cameras will be set up in places including, but not limited to, court side seating, mid-court seating and the baskets. These different camera locations will enhance the immersive experience for the users.

I think this collaboration will be highly successful because this event will serve the VR demographic – a young, tech-savvy audience. Additionally, many people do not have the ability to attend March Madness nor can they purchase court-side seats. However, with this creation the public will be able to access front row action from the comfort of their own couch.

Haifeng Zeng:

Virtual reality or virtual realities (VR), which can be referred to as immersive multimedia or computer-simulated reality, replicates an environment that simulates a physical presence in places in the real world or an imagined world, allowing the user to interact with that world. Virtual realities artificially create sensory experience, which can include sight, touch, hearing, and smell.

I think VR is very useful for soldiers, training pilot, and training driving and so on. It can simulate any situation and make the user feel real.

Alaina Chin:

It seems like amusement parks are upgrading their tech too because Six Flags just added a virtual reality roller coaster to their list of amazing rides! Six Flags teamed up with Oculus and Samsung to make this the first of its kind in North America where the riders experience fending off aliens while on the ride. It is called "The New Revolution" and provides a 360 view throughout the entire trip!

Can you imagine how awesome this ride is?! Roller coasters alone give you that adrenaline rush -- endorphins running high -- and now you're adding a new spin. You're playing the riders into a new world where not only is a visual given, but the fast turns and loops add to the experience, making you truly feel as if you're in a space craft of some sort, flying around! I can't wait to try this out next time I got to Six Flags!

Jasmine Blennau:

Virtual Reality headsets are on their way to becoming mainstream. In the article, "It Just Got Real," by Jane Zorowitz at NBC Sports Network, she profiles a company bringing VR to the professional sports world. When I first decided to research VR in sports, I thought about myself. I thought about sitting at home on my couch, putting on the headset and virtually transporting to floor seats at a Warriors game. It wasn't until later that I realized going to the Warriors game virtually could dramatically hurt ticket sales. The true way VR is infiltrating the sports market is not by creating the fan experience but creating the player experience.

According to the article, the company called STriVR Labs creates VR software for the Oculus that allows players to watch footage in a whole new way. Instead of watching on studying the opponent's plays in the screening room, players can experience plays through virtual reality. VR is being used to have athletes practice reading plays and making decisions virtually. The system designed by two Stanford graduates, uses real footage instead of video game style animation to place an athlete in a game like situation. The user even puts on equipment that records his or her biometric data to prove that they truly feel like they are experiencing the event.

The software can be applied to the NFL, NBA, NHL and college programs. It's taking off on the professional level. Even Bill Belichick is getting on board. That's something you can't ignore. So for someone who wants to work in professional sports, I am so in!

Aiden Daniels:

Violent video games have been controversial for as long as they existed. Whenever a heinous murder case or school shooting would happen, people would be quick to blame them (and/or movies, TV shows, music, or politicians they don't like.) Figures such as retired US Army Lt. Col. Dave Grossman refer to them as murder simulators, arguing that violent video games desensitize and teach children to kill people by virtually rewarding them for it. There has been one major flaw to this argument, however – the realism of the gameplay. Despite the talent of the best game developers, the most technologically advanced games really haven't been realistic – the gameplay and graphics were pretty abstracted and pretty easy to tell apart from reality. It's one thing to see gore in a video game, but when it comes to seeing it in *real life* – such as in crimes, car accidents, and war – that's *something else*. This, however, may change with the advent of technological advancement.

Products such as Occulus Rift are turning Virtual Reality from that thing we've dreamt of having as kids for our PS2s into a revolutionary game changer. As founder Tim Sweeney of video game development studio Epic Games comments, "You have an amazing ability to reproduce human emotion in VR." A particular game they are working with this in mind is the first person shooter *Bullet Train*. Bearing almost photographically realistic graphics and intense gameplay, it's said to create a frantic experience unseen in video games. As one journalist commented, he "broke a sweat… while wildly swinging two semi-automatic weapons" and "nearly cursed a few times, and aimed for the heads." "When it was all done," he wrote, "I was shaken. Did I really need a murder simulator?" He does not share these concerns alone, as video game developers Jesse Schell and Kimberly Voll worried about the long-term effects of this and that "it was only a matter of time before *Bullet Train* was blamed for a mass shooting."

Xi Ge:

Oculus is a very cool invention. With Oculus, people can experience the 3D images.

I think Oculus will be greatly used in the video games in the future. When the gamer put on the oculus, he will be in the world of the game. It seems that he is no longer a player, but a real person in that game. I know all the gamers like the feeling of being a part of the game. However, I am also worried about maybe these gamers may be so engaged to the oculus games that they can't separate the real life with the games.

Besides, oculus can be used to other fired, such as making cartons. I have seen a video on class that a man is creating the cartoon characters with the oculus. With the oculus, the carton looks more vividly. Also, we can draw the cartons in different angle. We can even turn around the carton to design the back of it. And then, a completely 3D image of a cartoon character will be done.

Shirley Nie:

I think that oculus rifts are a great invention because it allows people to interact with games in a 3D fashion. Not only does it upgrade the games from a 2D world only, it allows the players to fully immerse themselves into the game. I think that this is really cool and would be a huge thing for gamers and the like who would love this invention. However, I also think that it might be great to utilize these 3D oculus rifts for other things besides gaming such as drawing. I remember that in class, we watched a video where a Disney artist was drawing different characters from various Disney movies in the "zone" of the oculus rift. In addition, it would also help medical students a lot – imagine one day if they are able to scan a body into the oculus rift, such that a student would be able to perform several anatomy techniques on the virtual body rather than performing on actual bodies. I think that it will be super useful for other things besides only gaming. However, this is a great start into the world of 3D. I have no doubt that in the future, these goggles will become more and more accessible by people and the goggles will be upgraded several times as well. Probably in around five decades or so, there won't be a bulky pair of goggles but a sleek looking pair of glasses for the oculus rift instead.

Jared Oefelein:

As a college student, when I think about virtual reality I think about how it is going to change how we play games forever. Depending on who you are and what you do, you think about virtual reality in a different way altogether. If you are in the military, you might think about how virtual reality can prepare you for what may happen in the real world. That is what this video is all about. They talk about how the soldiers are training with VR and how the leaders will tell the people working the system to throw in something that the soldiers aren't expecting in order to see how they will react to this completely new scenario.

Jared Oefelein:

The Omni is designed to be a way for people to move around while using VR equipment. This solves the problem of how people can use VR and not run into walls while doing so. It keeps you in one place while you run, walk, jump, crouch, etc. This is incredible because now we have the virtual reality headset and we have the games for virtual reality and finally a place to use these things without either running into walls or sitting in a chair. The Omni adds the how immersive the virtual reality world can be. It will seem like you are somewhere else entirely. I am almost afraid that people will play too long and then try walking on the real floor and fall over. If you have ever run on a treadmill for a long period of time then you know what I'm talking about.

Jared Oefelein:

Augmented reality is different from virtual reality in the sense that it is not immersive. Augmented reality is basically taking what you see in the real world and altering it just a little bit in order to create an altered version of the world you live in. As opposed to virtual reality which is just taking the user and placing them in a totally new world, that may or may not have similarities to the world they live in, and it is full immersion.

We can use augmented reality in our everyday lives. For instance, we can use it to see what our houses would look like if we decorated a certain way. It would just use the camera on our phone to scan the room and then you could select what you want in the room and it will show you how it looks. Another application that might be possible is facial recognition software. It may be possible to spot criminals or tell if someone has committed a crime just by looking at them. The facial recognition would scan the face and then bring up background info on the person and warn the user if the person has any priors or if they are a known felon.

Jared Oefelein:

With full immersion virtual reality, the use of teachers becomes questionable. Using virtual reality we can explore ancient civilizations, interact with objects and manipulate them to see how changing one aspect effects how the object works, become part of a story or watch it unfold right in front of us with a narrator reading us the book simultaneously, ect. There are endless ways we can use virtual reality to teach students without the instruction of a teacher. With that in mind, should the people in the teaching profession start looking for other jobs? Do we need these people currently working to become teachers? Honestly I don't know. For all we know, virtual reality won't reach that point for a long time. As of today we definitely still need teachers in the classroom, but it's just a matter of time.

Jared Oefelein:

One of the most anticipated form of gaming is right around the corner and I couldn't be more excited. Virtual reality. Nothing has intrigued me more than VR gaming. It's one of those things that as a kid you hear about and you think that in the future everything will be done in VR, so you throw out a year such as 2012 and think that's going to be the future. Only, once 2012 comes around you are the only thing that changed and the world still looks like it did when you were a little child: No VR. Now, there have been breakthroughs in VR and what it can bring to the table for gaming. I only wish that I had the money to pay for it. I got a taste of VR when I went to New York Comic Con in October 2015 where they were letting people test the Oculus Rift. I paid twenty dollars to be able to dip my feet into the virtual world for the first time and it was incredible. They showed me some horror game whose title escapes me but I was mesmerized by how well it operated. It had some flaws but we are talking about virtual reality, so we can't expect it to be perfected already. I await the day where we have virtual reality similar to that of Sword Art Online, only less people should die.

Kenny Zhen:

Virtual Reality was only part of the imagination until the past 2 years or so. There were countless movies in the past in which the characters would be able to play a video game in virtual reality, or live in a virtual world; the most memorable one to me, is the Matrix.

But not, the technology to make virtual reality a real life concept is here. With it, things like the oculus (allowing people to explore a scene through visuals) virtual reality drawing (users are able to virtually draw with a wand like tool and walk through the object) and even virtual reality gaming is available. These advancements in technologies really makes one wonder to what extent will it take over our everyday lives? It was only 30 years ago, when the idea of a device that would be touch screen, allow you to communicate and see someone across the world, allow you to watch any video you desire, and even to answer any question, would be complete insanity. Now this is all possible through a cell phone and too many people, it has taken over their lives.

So to limit what virtual reality can do would be foolish. In my opinion, I am assuming that it will progress to the point where classrooms and lectures will be done through virtual reality; students can experience being in a classroom setting by sitting at home and putting on a contraption looking like a goggle. Not only this, but I can imagine medical experiments being performed by virtual reality, as well as virtual reality driving lessons, military training, pilot training and even virtual reality sports. Only time can tell what the future holds for this technology.

Chapter 2: The Impact of Technology on the Mind

Christopher Michael Esposito:

Recently, I took part in a discussion related to the current day's person's obsession with social media such as Instagram and Snapchat. Some say that these people crave attention by anticipating their "likes" and "views" on their posts, depending on whether they're using Instagram or Snapchat respectively. This led the discussion to move towards the topic of narcissistic personality disorder, and whether or not most people who use these social media are narcissistic. My contention is that these people are not narcissistic, but rather, egocentric instead.

As an infrequent Instagram and Snapchat user, I feel that obsessive social media users, who feel like it is a necessity to consistently update their peers with pictures and captions of their faces and the foods they're eating, have an innate desire to be the center of their own and their peer's universes at all times, and that, I feel, is egocentrism, and these social media only imbue its supporting personality traits.

Kenny Zhen:

Since the early 2000's, violent video games have become one of the most popular genres of video games. Games like Grand theft Auto, Call of Duty, Battlefront, God of War, Mortal Combat and Assassins Creed are just some examples of the most violent video games. These games contain brutal and gory killings, people being run over by cars and so much more. Due to this, the media has been antagonizing such video games for the past decade and has been advising parents to prohibit these kind of video games in their homes. Many have argued that being exposed to these video games will desensitize children to violence and even promote it as a response to stress or conflict.

I hold a very neutral perspective when it comes to this topic. On the hand, I do believe that the constant exposure to violence and gory killings can serve as a form of stimulation to children who are stressed. Such habits can potentially result in them acting it out in reality if a situation would arise where the child was involved in an altercation with another individual. Acts of woman abuse as portrayed in the Grand Theft Auto series can also potentially influence children to thinking that hitting and using women for sex is appropriate.

On the other hand, I believe violent video games can be an effective outlet for people to vent out their frustrations. It can also serve as a fun hobby. But with this, I believe proper teaching by parents is absolutely necessary. Parents need to inform their kids of the consequences of acting these things out in reality, as well as teaching their kids proper ways to release their anger.

Christina Dorf:

Taking the train home with a dead phone can be quite stressful and boring. Without a phone, what is there to do on a 2 hour train ride? I decided to spend my time observing my surroundings. I noticed that nearly every person was consumed in some form of technology; people watching videos on phones and tablets, people sending messages, people making phone calls, people taking selfies, and people with headphones in. One thing I did notice that almost seemed strange was that there was an older man on the train that was reading a paperback book. He stood out among the many people with their faces being lit up by glowing screens, and it was refreshing to see someone not so consumed by technology.

Christopher Michael Esposito:

Are current technological innovations good or bad? Technology always has its perks because it makes life easier. People are more productive, can multitask, and in some cases, don't even have to leave their comfortable homes to go to work. But, unfortunately, technology has its cons. Technological innovations yield a dependence like no other. People *need* these technologies to work, communicate, collaborate, and even to learn, do math, and spell as well.

From personal experience, when there is a blackout in a school or an office, the individuals who work there or are schooled there are free to go home, namely because the employees or teachers are helpless without their precious technological devices.

Another issue with such technologies is the competition that lies within the consumerism of these devices. Every person *must* have the newest, most convenient device out there, otherwise, the person who is outdated in his/her technology will become an outcast. Is this the right way to live? Should we be so materialistic?

Jakob Reilly:

Are we addicted to our phones? Last semester, several of my teachers challenged me to go an entire day - 24 hours - without technology. Their point in doing so was to show us just how dependent we have become on technology, and how we probably couldn't go an entire day without it. In fact, you were allowed to complete the assignment without going the entire day, provided you admitted that you couldn't do it. And while I didn't have too much trouble with the assignment - up until senior year I attended a summer camp that called complete abstinence from technology for an entire week - many of my peers really struggled with the assignment, because they couldn't get in touch with their friends and family. Many said they were lonely and just plain bored, and a couple gave up. Most spent the duration of the assignment in bed so that they didn't have to deal with it, usually totaling around twelve hours.

While I appreciate technology a lot - I use it just as much as the next guy, for need, convenience and entertainment - I also hold myself to being able to function and have fun without it. If I can't play on the computer? I'll read a book, or go out and play soccer, or basketball, or a board game. Computers are not the only way I can have fun. Yet people weren't able to survive without their phones, almost as if their lives had stopped until they could have them back. I think the logical assumption then is that people are losing the ability to think creatively. If any of these people had taken a moment of clarity to think what else they could do, they would have realized that they could have all grouped up and gone and played a sport. Or just studied with the text books they bought. And in general, they could do this on a regular basis, just interact with one another in person so that they can make that face time that creates deeper, more personal relationships.

Our phones have consumed us to where we would rather use our phones that interact with the people surrounding us. And while there are definitely benefits to using phones, we shouldn't be using them over getting to know other people that are near us.

Nonie Lee:

Have you ever had your phone in your pocket and felt a vibration, but when you checked your phone there were no messages or phone call? But you know you did feel a vibration, what could this be? Well it's called the Phantom Vibration Syndrome. This is because of a fear of someone trying to reach us. This shows how attached we are to technology. We can't do anything without our phones nowadays. It's our way of connected with people and because of that a lot of us probably have experienced this syndrome.

Just imagine in a few years our eyes might be glued to our phones. It doesn't even have to be a vibration. Have you ever had a time where you heard a ding and thought you got a message but when you checked your phone there was none? Because it turned out it was someone's next to you.

Patrick Wamsley:

My laptop is my baby. I don't anywhere without it. Every class and lecture, overtime I got hang out with friends, certainly every vacation and trip. How could I abandon my machine? What if I get a great project idea and have the urge to code for 12 hours straight (yes, that happens). What if I just get really board? My computer is the difference between me being fully engaged, productive and in the zone, and me being completely lost. About a year ago, I went a full day without my laptop. I'd like to say I did this as an experiment, to prove to myself that I could, but if I'm being honest, I left it in my girlfriend's car.

I survived, somehow. I find it fascinating how much we're all dependent on our machines (admittedly, some more than others). I spend upwards of 15 hours on my laptop per day, and I know that puts me at the end of the bell curve. But, don't most people spend at least a couple of hours on their computer, and another number of hours on their phone? And a few on the TV? It all adds up. A few generations ago, this wasn't true at all.

While technology is extremely helpful and revolutionary, it's important to remember that there is life outside that gorgeous 15" retina display. I'm trying to work on this.

Cynthia Hu:

I always picture myself checking my cellphone while walking and hit a tree or something. I mean, that never happens yet but I can see it happen. Still I like to constantly check my phone. And I see a lot of people on campus doing this. Sometimes I know I have nothing to do on the phone but I'll still unlock the screen, swipe around and lock it again. I'm not sure if it's caused by some kind of insecurity or something. Checking my phone every once in a while becomes a habit. Of course I miss the time when people only have that kind of keyboard phone that can only make phone calls and send text. But honestly I like the convenience smart phones and other technology brought us. But when it becomes too developed, it becomes something people rely on. Cell phone was invented because people can communicate easier this way. They can't carry phone around and they can't find payphone anywhere anytime. But now cell phone brought us way more than just convenient communication. It becomes a thing people use to avoid loneliness, awkwardness and all those feelings that they don't want to face directly. They choose to hide on their phone and stay in the imaginary world instead of facing the real world. I appreciate the advantages that technology brought us. It totally leads us to a brand new world. But on the other hand, people need to use these technologies in the right way.

Min-Ji Seo:

Most of the students in this school has their own laptop or desk top. Two years ago, I saw a girl playing League of Legend in the class. Because I don't play League of Legend, I didn't know whether she was good or not. However, I thought it was really disrespectful playing game in front of professor. I have a lot of friends playing league and I know now that how addictive it is. Even before League of Legend was first introduced, lots of people were addicted to Star Craft.

People commit a suicide because they think they can rebirth in real life like a game. They don't eat and sleep when they are in level-up phase. Playing computer games during their spare time is understandable. However, ill-judged play of computer games should be eradicated.

Gary Love:

The biggest distraction I have when I'm trying to get work done is my electronics. There's so much I can do on them and they're all at an arm's length of me at almost all times. I have to do a lot of my work on my computer. It's great that I have my computer to get work done on and stuff but it can also be a curse. I have games on my computer and a lot of times I will get an invite from a friend and I'll more often than not accept because I'd love a distraction from doing work. Work just isn't fun. Browsing the internet is. I can be looking through websites or articles online and before I know it I've wasted an hour that could've been spent on that essay due the next day. Writing this blog alone was a struggle because I kept getting distracted while writing it. My phone goes off because I get a text and the next thing I know I'm scrolling through every social media app I have. It just happens. I usually don't even realize how long I spend doing it. Technology is great and all and it can really help with getting work done easier, it can also make it take so much longer to do.

Maria Gomez:

I probably wouldn't be able to live without Instagram. That probably a really bad thing to say but it's the truth. I check Instagram every day, and if I ever skip a day I always scroll though my feed until I reach the last picture I saw the day before. Many people would say it's an unhealthy addiction, and I would probably agree, but it's come so natural to just check social media when you're bored or when you're avoiding responsibilities. It's a very effective way of getting insight of people's lives without actually having to communicate with them directly. People can share photos that they'd like other people to see. For me, it has become sort of like a portfolio of my life, including important events or just everyday photos of my life.

The people I follow range from people I went to high school with, to celebrities like Selena Gomez, Justin Bieber, and Beyonce. I like being able to see what celebrities are up to, as well as my friends who have gone away to college. It's like keeping up with everyone without actually talking to them. Of course I do talk to them but it's nice to see an actual photo of them with friends along with their phone verbal description. Instagram has become a useful part of my life, and I consider it as one of my favorite apps.

Ashley Villamar:

Communication is the sending and receiving of mutually understood symbols. Throughout history there have been several different styles of communication. For instance, the ancient Egyptians used hieroglyphics and Civil War troops used Morse code. With the rise of social media and advancements of smart phones, emoticons seem to be making a language of their own!

Almost all of my Facebook messages contain a few emoticons, stickers and GIFs. We are starting to communicate through visuals. Sometimes a photo or an emoji can better describe our feelings or reactions to a certain message or event. Although this is a fun way of communicating, I can't help but think that this may be a step backwards for social progress.

I think it's incredible important that we able to articulate and express how we feel through words. We cannot always rely on silly stickers and memes to express what we are thinking.

Jamie Mathew:

I don't really know how I used to live life before Google Drive, Calendar, or Keep. I've only been consistently using these features for two years or so but they have made my life so much easier. They allow me to organize my files, and my life as a whole, more conveniently than my actual computer does. It almost seems comical that my teachers in high school used to say we shouldn't save things by sending them to our emails because the internet might be down. Now, it's expected that everything is done on Drive. It is so much more manageable than a flash drive which I somehow always lost. No matter where I am, I always have access to my Google Drive. Google Calendar is so much better than a paper calendar. I can use it to manage my own day but I can also use it to keep track of other people in my life or find common free times to set meetings. And with its notifications, it makes me more disciplined about the schedule I set for the day. Google Keep is now my choice of electronic planner. It has a post-it note type feature that lets me color code and set labels so I can keep track of what I'm writing down. Plus I have it on both my laptop and phone so it's much more useful than a typical agenda. Google has electronized the most useful physical things that people use so that they don't need to carry around much more than their phone, tablet, and laptop. Everything I need is at the touch of a finger and it makes being a student that much easier.

Jamie Mathew:

One of the major reasons why there are so many cyberbullies in society today is that the bully can hide behind their computer screen. No one will ever know that a person is a bully because they are able to be anonymous, they don't have to attach a name or an identity along with their mean and hurtful comments. Websites such as Formspring make cyberbullying a major issue for adolescents. Formspring was a popular thing when I was in middle school and early high school. It is a website where people can post messages or questions for another person and it is usually done anonymously. I don't understand why websites like this exist because it is obvious that over time it is going to turn into a harmful environment. I also don't understand why a person would willingly sign up for websites like this. Not only are you giving bullies a space to post hurtful comments, but they are placing a target on their own back.

Shaniza Nizam:

I became an iPhone user about six months ago and one of the greatest things that I got from being an Apple user is read receipts. I have the ability to monitor when someone received my text and when they read. Of course, you can turn off read receipts so no one will know when you read it but most of my friends leave it on. This feature is great because when I send an urgent, time-sensitive message, I will know that the recipient got it and I don't have to stress. The feature is not so great because if someone is trying to blatantly ignore me, well I'll know they are. After about a month or two, a bunch of my friends turned off their read receipts and when I asked them why, they said, "Well, everyone else turned theirs off and I didn't want them to get my read receipts if I couldn't get theirs". I guess it's a give and take kind of thing, but I still kept mine on because it wasn't bothering me. Until I needed to avoid someone. Sometimes there are people who are annoying and you don't want to deal with but you have to deal with them. This was one of those cases and I was doing well ignoring that person and not clicking on the message but the moment I accidentally clicked on the message, they would know I read it and I would have to respond. I then realized how read receipts were a curse. Facebook has a similar feature on Messenger where you can see when someone has seen your message and although you can ensure someone got your time-sensitive message, you also can't effectively ignore someone because of this feature.

Shaniza Nizam:

All my friends are on Tumblr and for a while I was too until I realized it wasn't for me. I was interested in the funny gifs and the social empowerment side of Tumblr but all I came across was the dark, depressed side of it. I would follow other accounts full of what I was looking for but every sarcastic yet hilarious blog I encountered also had intense dark thought, memes and highly sexualized images. This was a common theme for Tumblr and although I understand that it was someone's personal blog and that was how they felt and they were entitled to put whatever they wanted on there, it wasn't for me. Everyone had posts and poems talking about how difficult and broken their lives and souls were and as a positive person, I could feel myself being dragged down by it.

Tumblr is full of emotions, and that is okay but when the predominant emotion is sadness and hopelessness and no one is making moves to fix that or help others through it, that's an issue. Toxic relationships filled with jealousy and greed were hypersexualized and idealized as if they were something we should all want. Although there are many dynamic, great things that have come out of Tumblr, there are some not-so-great things that have come out of there that we should address and use to help others.

Shaniza Nizam:

A few months ago a famous Instagrammer was all over the news because she was denouncing Instagram. She went back to all of her pictures and edited the captions to portray the reality behind the photo: the meals she skipped to achieve her look, the angles and editing she needed to look perfect. She caused huge waves in social media as many applauded her for speaking about adolescents and the need to appear perfect on social media. She denounced Instagram and urged others to stop using Instagram with her.

Although I find what she did admirable and am glad that she was finally able to live her truth, I think she needs to accept some responsibility for her actions. Saying that Instagram is the reason you lied and worked hard for likes and comments and followers isn't accepting her role in it. Social media is what we make it to be and yes, we sometimes need a wakeup call to remind us that Instagram isn't real life, but we also need to acknowledge our own actions.

Shaniza Nizam:

The other day my mom told me about a relative of mine who called her to brag about her children. This is nothing new, Bengali people (particularly those in my family friend circle) love to brag about their "perfect" kids like there's no children. Anyways, the relative told my mom about how her children were ranked the highest in their school and it was because they weren't allowed television, internet or phone. They focused on their studies and nothing would distract them. I expected my mom, a pretty straightforward, modern but not too modern woman to agree with the woman's methods but she didn't, to my surprise. She responded by saying "It's good that your kids are doing well but it's going to hurt them in the end. The whole world is relying more and more on technology and if your kids don't know how to use it or don't use it to their own educational advantage, they could end up behind in the end."

What my mom said was true, technology is here and no matter

how much we want to run in the opposite direction and go back to simpler times, it's just not possible. Depriving children of opportunities to understand the technology around them will hinder them later on when they will be expected to know how to utilize those same technologies. Of course, some children are given lots of access to technology and focus solely on the fun, not functional part of it and that is something that needs to be fixed: kids shouldn't rely on technology but they should know how to use it.

Joy Yim:

Through random browsing online, I've come upon so many inspirational websites that range from craft blogs to blogs of people who have gone through hardship and shared with the rest of the world about said hardship. I have been encouraged, inspired, and spurred to change little aspects about my life from this 'random browsing.' I know that popular websites like Pinterest and apartment therapy have affected many people's ideas for art and craft making, and this is something that the whole world should celebrate about. The sharing of ideas to make new ones. Through the World Wide Web this is made possible.

Joy Yim:

While I love all the convenience and various functions my smartphone provides for me today there is still a part of me that misses the days of my simple old flip phone. Even though my flip phone only allowed me to do use the basic call and text functions and really nothing beyond that there was a refreshing simplicity to just using a phone as a 'phone' and nothing else. I did not have the pressure of updating my social media accounts, which for most people today consists about more than three different social media accounts. I also didn't have the as many as distractions using a flip phone. My smartphone now has an endless amount of meaningless distractions which I get caught up playing with and wasting hours of my day with. For example I can stay on my Instagram app for hours, without getting bored and to say that Instagram is a waste of time is an understatement. There really is not much of any use for Instagram for the daily activities of life other than to see the perfected pictures of other people's lives. During my flip phone days, I spent the time I use now spending on my smartphone on other activities like going outdoors or instead making the effort to see other friends face to face instead of just 'snapping them pictures' or messaging them on one of the many messaging apps. While the convenience of my smartphone does save time in terms of communication with friends, family, and the rest of the world it also wastes the limited time we have endless distractions. I do love my smartphone but sometimes I crave the days when I didn't have the pressure to check my phone every few minutes. I miss the simpler days but I also love having the opportunity to tap into the world of people in another culture than mine.

Shirley Nie:

Online dating has become so popular lately, where people meet other people online and then where they go on from there is what they decide. There's no commitment, no danger (granted if the other person is not a psychopath or something similar) and guilt free. At first, people considered Facebook as an online dating site but now, it has become something universally used by people of all ages to get updates from friends. Now, Okcupid or tinder has become the new dating website/ mobile apps where many people log in and see they will like to meet. Majority of the time, these sites are used for hooking up and not really for meeting new people. Of course, meeting new people and finding the love of your life is possible but it is rare. Personally, I've never used any online dating websites because I don't like the idea of people judging you mostly on your looks and swiping left or right. In addition, you do not know who you are meeting so there is a huge risk on your part. They can possibly be a mass murderer, another Ted Bundy on the loose – you just don't know. Also, who the person is online can be different from the person you meet in real life. When you have high expectations of the person and you meet them in real life, they can be different from what you imagine them to be and the blow can be just as hard. Maybe I'm traditional, but I would prefer meeting people in real life than meeting them across the screen.

Christopher Michael Esposito:

Her- a movie that accurately depicts the near future of lonely love. The movie describes the future of artificial intelligence and how it can innovate one of the few precious things that not even science can explain- relationships. It describes the quirky development of a relationship between a man and an operating system.

For the most part, the relationship works, but unfortunately, the movie does unveil the harsh truth behind heartless machinery; it can't love like we love. It is a shame that this movie does, indeed, describe the direction technology is moving in, and hopefully, this genius director's foresight opens the eyes of some of the commoners in our society.

Christopher Michael Esposito:

A pressing question in today's progressive, innovative society is do new technologies help people for the better or the worse? We know that technology is beneficial to society's progression, but does it help the people? I believe that it greatly impairs the social skills of most people. For example, how can a person that is busy toggling with his social media communicate with his peers in a social setting?

Oftentimes my social interactions with my friends will consist of speaking about recent Facebook or twitter posts, therefore, refraining from speaking about important topics and only focusing on trivial, picayune gossip. I don't see the productivity in such social interactions. This leads to a novel question do new technologies reduce the productivity of physical, social interactions? If so, how could this be fixed?

Yulia Huertas:

Selfies everywhere. I think with time, the image of how a woman is expected to look in a picture or what's deemed beautiful has changed. New facial expressions have been introduced and now seem "cool." People on social media put up a front, in a sense, to look visually pleasing to the world. I too have contributed to this. I only post my best looking photos that I like on my social media. But, with social media created with the intent to create, share and exchange information, is what we see visually, really what is true?

Meme's have also become a popular visual representation of

social media. A meme, is "a humorous image, video, piece of text, etc. that is copied (often with slight variations) and spread rapidly by Internet users." Many times, meme's poke fun at trends popular within today's culture. Going back to selfies and women, I found a meme trending on the explore page of my Instagram.

I laughed... because it's sort of, kind of, true. With the introduction of Snap Chat to the social media world, the culture of selfies changed. There's something about Snapchat camera that makes someone look better. The added face recognizing filters gave an additional embellishment to the photo. The most popular, the dog filter. To me, it's all funny to see.

I also think meme's have allowed us to express our thoughts and beliefs better via social media and messaging. We can visually see the expression and link it back to a thought. Definitely something that changed the game of the visual culture on social media.

Shirley Nie:

Although I've never been in long distance relationships before, from what I've heard from friends, it seems to be hard and never long-lasting. It would always start off with both people promising to talk every day, Skype every day or message each other every day. However, as they meet new people and encounter difficult classes, there will be less time for other person and vice versa. Slowly conversations slowly die or they slowly only center around work. Then, eventually they realize that it won't work and break it off. However, what if we had something like holograms or robots that were the other person. Not only does it give the comfort of the other person being there, it will probably help the relationship last longer. Not only for relationships, but it can strengthen family ties especially if half your family lives across the world. For example, I know that my parents would love to use it to talk to their friends that are all in China. I would love to use it to talk to my friends that are all scattered across the United States. I think it would definitely work to help relationships last since the other person will be there "in spirit", except in robot form.

Jared Oefelein:

When it comes to long distance relationships, technology has made it incredibly easy to stay in touch with your significant other. With the help of smart phones, people are able to text and call each other on a daily basis. What if you just want to see them? Well then you can use Skype to call them on your laptop, phone or game console. Skype allows you to video chat with other people from all over the world. As long as you are awake when they are, accounting for the time difference, you can see your significant other whenever you like. Thanks to technology we are able to keep our relationships going even when we have be apart for extended amounts of time. Then when you finally get to see each other, it's almost like you never left. Almost. Technology can't hug people for you but, hey, maybe soon?

Jared Oefelein:

I don't know about anyone else but even if I am not expecting a text/call/email/notification on my phone, I still find myself checking for one every couple of minutes. When I am expecting one it's worse because I get anxious thinking that I might miss it or maybe I got the notification already but it was with a mess of other notifications as well so i didn't notice it. It sometimes takes up my entire life. I'll just sit around waiting for the notification to come and if it doesn't I just wasted all that time waiting for nothing. Sometimes I feel like my life was better without a phone and that I got more things done. Then I remember that when I didn't have a phone I would avoid my responsibilities by playing video games or drawing. So there's that. Although doing those things still counts as a hobby. One of my main hobbies now is checking my phone for notifications. I feel like I need a break from being connected. I think we all should take a break.

Jared Oefelein:

There are people who believe that playing video games for too long is bad for you, that it destroys your eyesight, or that it increases antisocial behaviors. These people are wrong. As an avid gamer myself, I have done some research on the topic and found that not only are these people wrong but the opposite is true. Video games are good for you. It was found that by playing a Mario game for thirty minute a day for an extended amount of time you are developing parts of your brain that deal with memory, problem solving and spatial awareness. Furthermore, it had been shown that by playing Call of Duty the player's eyesight is trained to see difference in shade and movement better than the average person who does not play. As for the people saying that gaming causes mental illness, they too are wrong. Video games can actually be used as a one on one therapeutic activity that can help the people struggling with mental illness. So when someone belittles your gaming hobby, just clue them in on the benefits of what you are doing.

Nikki Fogarty:

I believe that most people have an addiction to technology and you're lying if you say you don't. Most people couldn't leave their dorm or house without their phone, and if they did they would feel lost. I didn't realize hoe addicted I was to my iPhone until I had to give apple my phone for an hour and a half for it to be fixed, in that hour and a half I was lost and I didn't know what to do. With this being said, I feel like I should try and fix my addiction, and try to put my phone away at times, but it's going to be a slow fix.

Lily Yuan:

I'm addicted to my email. Every moment that I'm free I open the app and refresh, hoping to see a new email or two. I'm not looking for anything in particular; I just crave the next quick fix of opening and reading a new email. This is how a typical day may go.

8AM: Wake up, check my email. No new messages
9AM: Come back from a shower, one new message from Handshake.
10AM: Open the gmail app while running to class late, nothing new.
10:20AM: In the middle of class and bored. One new email from Handshake.
11:20AM: Casually strolling to the next class while opening the app, one new email from my club.
1PM: Lunch time. One new email responding to the previous email from the club.
1:01PM: A flurry of emails arrives, all responding to the previous

email responding to the previous email from the club.

2PM: Inactivity from the app

3PM: Email from my major department head

3:30PM: New email from Handshake.

4PM: Nothing new

5PM: Nothing new

6PM: Still nothing

7PM: Same old, same old.

8PM: Spam email from online shopping website

9PM-12PM: Sudden burst of productivity while doing homework. Email app currently being ignored.

1PM: One last check at the good ole email app before bedtime.

Chapter 3: Biomedical Engineering

Stephanie Hahn:

Unlike Fitbit and the Apple watch that does not provide user's health on a molecular level, smart wristbands and headbands embedded with swear sensors could sync data wirelessly in real time to smartphones using Bluetooth.

This technology is useful because sodium and potassium in sweat could help check for problems such as dehydration and muscle cramps. Glucose can keep track of blood sugar levels. Lactate levels can keep track of blood flow problems and skin temperatures.

Bridget Scheinert:

The VR has really made a name for itself in the science world. Between building proteins and surgical training it has become a huge part of what is to come for VR in the sciences. In a new game call InCell the VR takes you inside a cell. This is very beneficial for several reasons. One reason is that it allows scientists to be able to manipulate certain organelles within the cell and possibly see the effect it has on cells that are reproduced from it. This is major in the science industry for drug development and possible cure for diseases.

Bridget Scheinert:

Genome sequencing brings major advancements to the science world. There are both positive and negative outcomes of genome sequencing. Gene sequencing can allow for the discovery of specific diseases early in one's life. This allows people to take the necessary precautions and possible early treatments to either control or cure their disease. Besides disease discovery it also allows people to know if they will have a disease later on in life and what can be changed or altered to possibly cure their disease. The negatives of genome sequencing greatly stem from superficial views. Many are scared that if our genomes are sequenced and parents are given the opportunity to change how their unborn child looks that our world will turn to one that is not diverse. This is a negative effect on genome sequencing however i think there will be government control before it becomes too extreme. The positives of genome sequencing greatly outweighs the negative effects that come with it.

Klaudia Ciszewska:

Being a pre-med student I like to be updated on all of the advances going on in medicine. There have been many discoveries about how 3d printing can be involved in many situations. Before, the only way someone could get a new organ was through a transplant from another person, now we have come far as to be able to 3d print human organs with necessary stem cells that work exactly the same as human organs. Scientists are developing ways to be able to 3D print bones, blood vessels and hearts among others. The future of medicine relies very heavily on technology now and has come very far from medicine back then.

Shirley Nie:

What if in 50 years, instead of binding two people in marriage with wedding rings, we utilize neuro-sensors? Whereas wedding rings will allow you to just state your claim on the other person, these neuro-sensors will tell you where your spouse is and what your spouse is feeling at all times. As for me, I would hate these limiting neuro-sensors. There will be no privacy and individuality in the relationship. In addition, a relationship is built on trust and love. If my spouse had all access to my feelings and thoughts, then I think that all the years of building the relationship would disappear. No longer would I be able to think on my own, I would have to think for another person too, and thinking alone is difficult as it is. If these neuro-sensors were to become a trend in the future, I suppose that I will not get married at all.

Chanpreet Singh:

Many people don't see coding and biology as going together. The only instance anyone probably heard of is, DNA coding, which is not exactly done in Java or MATLAB. But soon, you will find that these two components are going to be intertwined. The reason is, coding aids both diagnosis and research of medical diseases. Scientist and Doctors can use codes to analyze a patient's medical report quicker and cross reference with previous cases to more efficiently treat patients. In the same way, doctors are currently using coding constructs to study tumors and determine the stage, drug resistance and prognosis of cancer in patients. This task is usually extraneous and time consuming: going through each line of DNA and find a mutation or similarity between other cancers. But codes and computer can do this thousands of times faster and more accurately.

Andy Law:

With the recent hype around quantum computing, many have missed out on another form of computing, bio-computing. However, this is to be expected due to the vastly different use of bio-computing. This type of computing uses organic molecules to represent transistors in a processors, much like how DNA and proteins work. In a way, it is similar to how brains conduct and send electrical impulses through neurons in order to represent information.

The development of bio-computing offers a unique perspective on computing. Bio computers are made of specially engineered bio-material. Over time this material can grow and adapt to the data it processes and possibly even mimic the creative processes us humans have, possibly giving it a consciousness and allow it to do creative work. Normal computing lacks the ability to think creatively since it only knows how to calculate information. Essentially normal computing is the computer that when to an engineering-science school while bio-computing is the computer that decided to go to a liberal arts school.

Dionis Wang:

The development of neuro-sensors is still mostly for professional use. One type of neuro-sensor, the EEG, is a device that has the ability to measure electrical activity of the user's brain. By wearing a cap the EEG can this data to allow for manipulation and use. The use of the EEG is shifting to more entertainment and being introduced to gaming. In this aspect it is even lesser known than the Oculus Rift and could be said to be at the infancy age in the realm of gaming. The EEG is being introduced to developers in hopes that games and other apps will be created and will push the development of the EEG to the next level.

In class Professor Baldwin showed us the EEG he has and the different projects he is involved in. The EEG worked and responded to changes in facial expression of Professor Baldwin and displayed this brain activity on the screen. His project's goal is to use these data and produce music corresponding to the brain activities. In class the demonstration showed that when Professor Baldwin changed this facial expression the speed of the random note being play will change. When more facial muscle were tense there is an increase in speed and when the facial muscles were more relaxed there is a decrease in speed.

The use of EEG is still in its infancy and as long as developers keep working new programs will come out and improve. One day playing a game with just your thoughts might not be impossible anymore. Like the Oculus Rift technology the EEG can be developed into games given time.

Nikki Fogarty:

Being someone who has worn glasses since the 5th grade, and contacts since the 9th grade, I wish I had perfect vision like my peers. Waking up in the morning and not being able to see the clock that is 5 feet away is a struggle that I have to deal with every day. Without having my glasses on, or contacts in I am blind to the world. One way that I could fix this problem is laser eye surgery. This is something that I wish I could do but there are two problems. One, I'm only 18 and it's recommended that you be 21 to get this surgery. Second, this surgery is very expensive and insurance doesn't cover it. I wish that insurance covered it just like they cover so many other things. Although this surgery is something really scary, being that they basically cut you eye ball, it's something that I want to happen in the future, so I can see myself saving up and punching this.

Lily Yuan:

Bioengineering is an amazing up-and-coming field. It has only started to come into prominence due to the advancement of modern medicine and technology. It combines these fields together, along with the classic training of engineering to allow people to build devices to suit medical needs. As the future gets filled with more and more technology, and has an increasingly older population, solutions to medical problems can be made to make care of elderly patient easier. It can also be used to help reduce current disease levels, and to find a cure for diseases that may not have a cure. Genetic engineering, a specific subset within biomedical engineering, seeks to alter gene structure itself in order to solve these medical problems.

Nikki Fogarty:

In the past hundred years the advancement in medical equipment has helped many people in numerous of ways. Now there have been many new ways to determine what exactly is wrong with the patient faster. With this advancement it will save lives because if someone needs a certain medicine right away, a faster medical equipment will give them the answers of what medicine is needed. Also advancements in the medical medicine itself has helped people in many ways. In the next hundred years I believe that the medical equipment would advance further and hopefully we will find more cures to certain problems.

Betty Monsanto:

While watching an episode of VICE on HBO "Beating Blindness/ White Collar Weed Ep. 4" I learned about a blind man who underwent surgery with a retinal implant to restore "useful" vision. The device is a pill size device that goes in and around the eye paired with glasses and video camera. The restore vision would give the patient visuals of black and white shapes that would serve useful for everyday travel.

Lily Yuan:

3D printing is an amazing invention due to its varied applications. It has been used to replication hard to find plastic figures, custom-make and print designs, and other fun things. It can also be used seriously as a way of treating patients with improperly working body parts. The 3D printer can be used to make a replication of the correct working part, which can then be inserted into the patient. There was recently a story of a patient that received a 3D printed component of the spine, during which a 12+ hour operation was performed to remove the portion of the patient's actual spine and insert the printed component in. This treatment was a success, indicating that 3D printing has a future in medical applications. Maybe even one day, more complex structures can be built, such as kidneys, which currently has many people on the waiting list, waiting for a donor.

Min-Ji Seo:

When you watch the sci-fi movie, sometimes, you will see a person with modified gene who is charming and smart. Not far from now, we might have kids whose gene is modified. Last year, CRISPR-Cas 9 technology was developed to modify gene. It uses the characteristic of bacteria to modify the gene. We can get rid of gene that we don't need and insert the gene that we want to express into human or other organism's DNA. However, this technology brought the big ethical issue. Few days ago, England allowed the gene modification using CRISPR-Cas 9 even though there is still issue going on. Human still don't know the role of all the gene and component of the body. We also don't know how they interact. Therefore, knocking out one gene might not mean knocking out one phenotype. Knocking out one gene on you might cause deafness and blindness at the same time. There in my opinion, it is too early to start the gene modification since we don't know everything about our body yet. However, after the fully understanding of our body, doing experiment on gene modification will give more positive effect that negative effect on human.

Minghui Lin:

In the videos, it's about one Neuro-headset product named Emotiv Insight. When I first watch this video, I am very interested and excited. I have been interested about this kind of neuro technology for a while. The world is about data. So does human-being. I was thinking that if there are any ways to store human thinking data as soon as we are able to detect their mind-wave in the future. So far, we can detect mind-wave by wearing this kind of handset. Depend on these data, we can analyst our emotion from them. Thus, in the future human may be able to lie under these headset machine. This is similar to Polygraph that can detect if human lies. There kind of machines are very helpful for market in the future. People who wear this headset can be tracked. Their emotion and interesting can be detected and analyst. In the future, the handset may be made smaller and smaller which is like personal computer. People may just wear on their ear and connect to anything in anywhere. For example, connect this handset to phone, and then use detected mind-wave to control phone automatically. Right now, this headset only has input for itself. In the future, they may have output to human being. Of course, they may be able to animal or plants. Then we may be available to communicate with them. These are very excited for me. I am getting very interested to know about more them. I wish that I could contribute as much as I can for this technology. I probably can start up a business based on this.

Chapter 4: Technology and Therapy

Alaina Chin:

Recently, hospitals have started implementing virtual reality "treatment" for patients who are stuck in the hospital for long periods of time. Studies have shown that after 90 days of being kept in a pretty repetitive lifestyle, where the patient spends the majority of their day in bed and only sees the few same nurses, a person can become less motivated and overall start going into vegetable-like states, as seen with patients who have extended hospital stays for severe illness/injuries.

By using virtual reality simulations, it eases the patient's mind by alleviating any psychological or physiological stress and lets him or her escape the confines of his or her hospital room. Hopefully, this becomes a nation, if not worldwide, application of virtual reality.

Andy Law:

Under Iron Man's technological masterpiece of an exoskeleton lies Tony Stark, who asides from being super smart is a human being. His exoskeleton gives him insane abilities such as making him super strong, giving him the ability to fly, etc.

While the story of Iron Man may be fake the technology he uses to create his suit is slowly becoming a reality. Panasonic recently developed an exoskeleton which would allow Japanese workers to lift heavier loads while protecting their back. This is one of the first cases of using machine augmentations to assists in human actions. Panasonic is taking steps into uncharted territory, as this suit has both potential to change people's lives. If exoskeletons become a normal thing, things such as lifting heavy objects with forklifts may not be needed. It could even help those suffering from body weakening diseases such as Cerebral Palsy with their illness, giving them the support they need.

On a darker note however, the exoskeletons could also be used in war. Given enough time to develop us could one day see military forces armed with exoskeletons that turn them into super humans, giving them the ability to take bullet shots, run at extremely fast speeds etc.

Shaniza Nizam:

Technology that can help blind people make some sort of sense about their spatial location in a room and the objects around them sounds amazing and innovative but in reality, it is highly unlikely that this will ever be created. First of all, turning all of the objects and their relative distances into sounds would absolutely overwhelm the person using the new technology. Because they are already extremely sensitive to their sense of hearing, the various sounds of the surroundings would bombard the person.

Another issue is that there is always something in your background and foreground, so you would always have the technology making noise and not really giving a clear distinction between the changing objects in the background and foreground.

Laura Dominguez:

According to the American Music Therapy Association, music therapy is the clinical and evidence-based use of the music interventions to accomplish individualized goals within a therapeutic relationship by a credentialed professional who has completed an approved music therapy program. There have been lots of studies saying that adolescents obtain many benefits from listening to music, including emotional, social, and daily life benefits and it also helps forming their identity. It has been scientifically proven that music can improve an adolescent's mood by reducing stress and lowering anxiety levels, which can also help by preventing depression. Listening to music can also help you with heart disease and neurological disorders such as amnesia, dementia and Alzheimer's.

Marissa Bavaro:

I watch a lot of Youtube videos on makeup and such, and I always found it so interesting that so many "beauty gurus" claim to have anxiety and other psychological issues. The person that I selected for this blog post is Kathleenlights; she discusses how she struggles with anxiety. In high school she had a small group of friends that weren't that popular-- they used to eat lunch in a classroom with their favorite teacher. She got married at 18 because her husband is in the military. She isn't the only beauty Youtuber I have watched that also struggles with anxiety. Once I started noticing that so many had anxiety problems, I started wondering why that was the case.

Well, it was obvious once I really thought about it. Their full time occupation is to sit in an empty room in their house and talk to a camera. It's not that Youtube is causing them to have more anxiety, it's just that people who have anxiety and social problems tend to choose the occupation of making videos on Youtube. In my opinion, they seem to be getting more anxiety this way though because people are so mean on social media; the comments on their videos are probably causing them more anxiety than a job in the outside world would. There is one Youtuber I watch named Nikkie Tutorials and she always discusses how Youtube is so hard for her because she loves people and being around people, so sitting in front of a camera by herself is not fun for her. Hearing her say that made it that more clearly to me why people who struggle with anxiety choose to make Youtube videos.

Bridget Scheinert:

The VR has many uses especially in the medical field. One way virtual reality is being used in the medical field is to deal with anxiety through meditation. A recent app called DEEP trains users in how to breathe deeply allowing them to properly meditate. It requires that breathing be the only way to control when playing the game. This is beneficial to a wide variety of people because those who are unable to use the joystick for whatever reason can still participate because breathing is the only requirement, and everyone needs to breath.

Bridget Scheinert:

After people lose a limb they experience extreme pain from their no longer attached appendage. Some treatments for phantom limb pain is mirror therapy in which patients stare at a mirrored image of their still attached limb and trick their brain into feeling the movements as if they still had their other limb. The patient uses virtual reality to complete tasks as if they had all limbs attached giving relief to the brain by tricking it into feeling like it has all limbs. Sensors are also attached and sense the nerve impulses coming from the brain.

Bridget Scheinert:

Virtual reality can be used for many different things including medicine. In a study done by the University of Louisville it was seen that the VR could be used in situations where people are trying to overcome their fears. An example of this is people who are afraid of flying. The VR allows people to simulate a flying experience while being in a controlled environment. It can also be used in cases where people are claustrophobic. The one thing that is very convenient about using VR to overcome fears is that it can be done privately in a controlled environment that allows for the patient to use it one day at a time.

Maria Gomez:

Using devices for blind people to help them see using different wavelengths could be a very helpful innovation. However, it may not work for everyone when you take into account the problems that are evident in the use of it. Not all people see the same things differently, so it would be difficult to create something that helps a person see when there really is no set perspective of looking at things. In addition, the device could malfunction and not be an effective tool, and some people would just simply be against using it. I personally think it would be helpful, but I wouldn't blame anyone who wouldn't want to use it. Blind people have their other senses heightened, including hearing, and to have a constant buzzing noise directly in your ear all day would be extremely annoying. However, it is great technology that is becoming available for disabled people.

Christopher Michael Esposito:

Today I watched a very interesting video in my theater class.

The video consisted of various people trying on the HTC Vive, a virtual reality device, while having to save a cat that's sitting outside a skyscraper, only to be supported by a wooden board. To make things interesting, the participants in this game/demonstration were required to stand on a wooden board (in actual reality) and save a stuffed animal that is placed at the end of the board in actual reality as well. The participants thought the game was all too real. They started screaming and wobbling, as they would do if they were actually in this situation.

This video demonstration captivated my interest because I believe that such a realistic life simulator, like the Vive could be used for some kind of psychological therapy. In the case of the cat on the wooden board demonstration, the device seems like it would be a good fit for people suffering from post-traumatic stress disorder (PTSD). I also believe that it may be a good fit for individuals with autism. In psychological treatments for autism, researchers often use interactive computer paradigms to assess their social skills, why not uses a virtual reality device instead to get a more realistic assessment of their social skills?

Micah Baja:

In today's day in age technology surrounds us. Whether or not you think it is good for humanity or not, you cannot escape it. From cellphones, to TVs, security cameras, and even watches, technology is a daily given. It may even seem too much as if it is suffocating, but there is a silver lining. Technology today is being used in major therapeutic sciences.

One direct way it can be seen in therapy is to better understand the patient and his/her problems with an EEG. This device is used to read and record brain waves as the brain reacts while the client using the device is conscious. This device can help doctors understand what goes through a patient's brain while they are being reviewed. This works by corresponding brain waves to certain feeling and reactions that are felt. This can further research and hopefully lead doctors down the right path to improvements in research.

Ricardo Dixon:

In the past decade there has been a massive progression in the advancement of technology. The thought of this phenomenon is so intriguing because of its fast track evolution and expansion. Only about twenty years ago was when the resurgence of 3-Dimensional aspects like movies and games were readmitted into the world of public consumerism, but now technology has journeyed into an entire different world. Recently there has been the introduction of virtual reality entertainment, literally a completely different world where everything is virtually encrypted to parallel real life sequences. This realm has been alluring to innovators in every field ranging from medical, travel, entertainment, educational etc. They're looking of ways to utilize the world of virtual reality via headsets like the HTC Vive to further progress their fields of interest. The idea that this advancement in technology is making the lives of humans much easier, especially when correlated to the progression in human development in health.

Virtual reality has many functions to where it can be a crucial asset to any field, but one in particular is for its therapeutic simulations. VR can be utilized for humans to overcome their phobias or even rehabilitate skills that they have possibly lost. For instance, VR exposure therapies can help people who have a fear of heights by injecting them into a virtual simulation of them being hundreds of feet in the air, asking them to complete a task while being exposed to the setting. Another instance per say is for a person who suffers from PTSD (Post Traumatic Stress Disorder). After say being in a car accident a person may be scared to drive because they were traumatized, the VR has the ability to simulate them driving a car and fully rehabilitate them back to their normal selves. The utilization of virtual reality in therapeutic settings are endless, they are bound to have a great influence on human development in health in the years to come.

Editor's Note

Written by Christopher Michael Esposito

As I stated earlier in the Preface, there is an interesting juxtaposition that is characterized throughout many of these blogs, particularly in the second and fourth chapters, when discussing the impacts of current technologies on social skills.

Many of the blog posts in the second chapter discuss the students' complaints about their cell phones consuming their lives for an array of reasons, but mostly texting anxiety. One blog post even describes an interesting phenomena called phantom vibration syndrome, which occurs when a person believes that he or she feels a vibration, indicating that he or she received a text, but actually did not. This example was used to explain the anxiety that is bestowed upon the users of these current technologies, which couples with unfortunate social deficits as well.

Contrarily, the fourth chapter discusses the potential for current technologies to be used as means to enhance socialization. Two examples immediately come to mind. One blog describes how interactive computer games are being used to aid the social deficits that are often seen in individuals with autism. Another example can be found when the HTC vive is used to treat the anxiety of people who suffer from PTSD.

This underlying contrast that is seen throughout the second and fourth chapters of the book is useful to know for two reasons. First, it shows that there will always be pros and cons to every technological advancement. And second, that there is amazing potential in all the current technologies, it just depends on how the people decide to utilize them.

Index

Glossary

Augmented Reality (AR)- a composite image of the user's vision as well as an immersive three dimensional computer generated image.

Biomedical Engineering (BME)- an area of study that seeks to develop biomedical tools with the aid of technology.

Therapy- a form of treatment that helps relieve a negative symptom of impairment.

Social Media- all websites and applications that allow users to share content or take part in social networking.

Virtual Reality (VR)- an immersive, three dimensional image generated by a computer that may seem so real that it can seemingly be detected by all human senses, not just sound and/or sight alone.

www.ingramcontent.com/pod-product-compliance
Lightning Source LLC
Chambersburg PA
CBHW051212050326
40689CB00008B/1283